Skills for
SCHOOL
SUCCESS

Written by Meg Greve

Content Consultant
Taylor K. Barton, LPC
School Counselor

Rourke
Educational Media

rourkeeducationalmedia.com

Scan for Related Titles
and Teacher Resources

www.rourkeeducationalmedia.com

PHOTO CREDITS: Cover, page 16-17: © fstop123; page 4, 5: © Steve Debenport; page 7: © Mark Bowden; page 8: © Carmen Martínez Banús; page 10: © Silvia Jansen; page 11: © Marilyn Nieves; page 12: © Linda Yolanda; page 13: © Margot Petrowski; page 14: © Kim Gunkel; page 15: © Jaren Wicklund; page 18: © kali9; page 20, 22: © GlobalStock

Edited by Precious McKenzie

Cover and Interior Design by Tara Raymo

Library of Congress PCN Data

Skills for School Success / Meg Greve
(Social Skills)
ISBN 978-1-62169-904-0 (hard cover) (alk. paper)
ISBN 978-1-62169-799-2 (soft cover)
ISBN 978-1-62717-010-9 (e-Book)
Library of Congress Control Number: 2013937299

Rourke Educational Media
Printed in the United States of America,
North Mankato, Minnesota

Also Available as:

rourkeeducationalmedia.com

customersevice@rourkeeducationalmedia.com • PO Box 643328 Vero Beach, Florida 32964

TABLE OF CONTENTS

WELCOME TO YOUR NEW JOB!

You may not have a real job that pays real money, but right now, school is your job. You have to be there on time every day, come prepared to work, follow directions, and work with other people. This book is a tool for you to be the best student you can be.

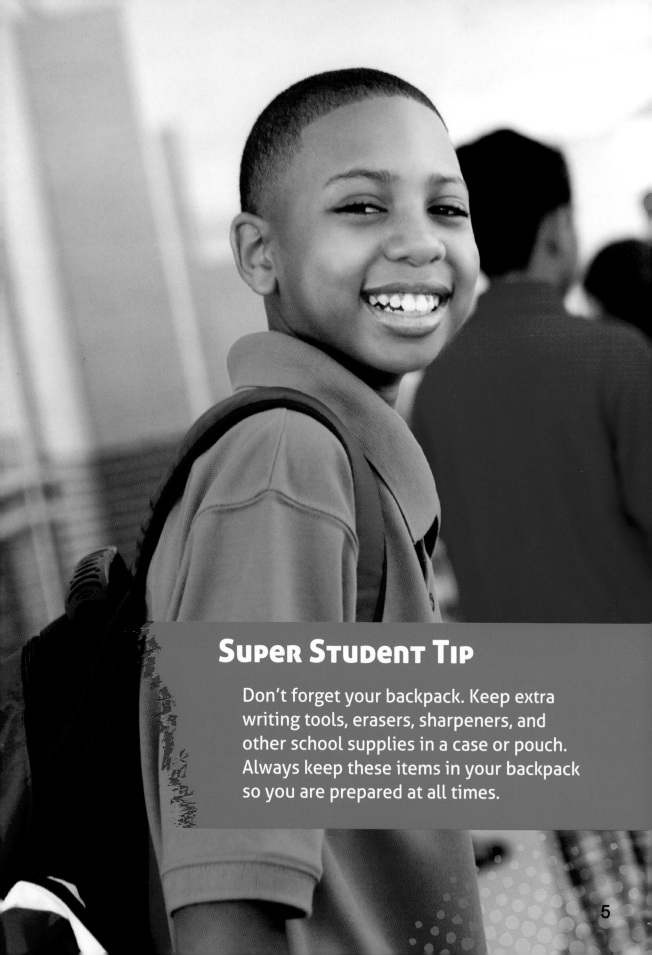

Super Student Tip

Don't forget your backpack. Keep extra writing tools, erasers, sharpeners, and other school supplies in a case or pouch. Always keep these items in your backpack so you are prepared at all times.

Put People on Your Team

School may feel hard at times, so that is why you want to have lots of people on your team. The first person you should use as a **resource** is your teacher. Always talk to your teacher when you are confused or worried about classwork.

Other important people you need on your team are your parents. Let them know about problems you might be having and the successes too. It is always best to let them know how things are going so they can support you.

Older brothers and sisters may be annoying, but they are the perfect people to help you with math problems, to study for a test, or to read a report before you turn it in. Who knows, you might be able to help each other!

Super Student Tip

Be sure to ask a grown-up if you need to find out facts and information on a computer. Teachers and parents know how to direct you to the information you need so you stay safe online.

GOAL SETTING

In school, you don't have to kick a ball into a net to win. All you have to do is set **goals** for yourself and work to achieve them. Goals can be as simple as getting a good grade on a spelling test, or as complicated as completing a science fair project.

Cool School Tool

Use this table to help you create a plan to meet your goal.

Reward yourself when you reach your goal.

It can be something easy like some extra relaxation time,

or having a friend over to listen to music.

Goal	
When do I need to meet this goal?	
What materials or resources do I need?	
Who will help me if I get stuck or need some extra help?	
What will I do to meet this goal?	
When I do meet this goal . . .	

9

HOMEWORK HELPERS

Studying hard and practicing hard will help you reach your goals and make a few too!

Getting organized and meeting the homework challenge can help you achieve success in school. Homework is meant to give you extra time to practice what you have learned in school.

Get a homework folder and put all of your homework and assignments in it. Also, keep a calendar in your folder so you can write down assignments and their due dates.

Super Student Tip

Check your homework notebook. Do you have any long-term assignments or goals you need to work on? Make a list of what you need to get done. Start with assignments due tomorrow, or tests you have to take in the next few days. Once you finish one of the items on the list, cross it off. You will feel great once your list is all checked!

When you get home, take a break. Have a snack and relax for a few minutes. Then it is time to get started. Don't wait too long. The longer you wait, the harder it is to get started.

Make sure you have a quiet place to do your homework. Use your room, or another quiet room that is free of distractions like phones, video games, and annoying little brothers or sisters!

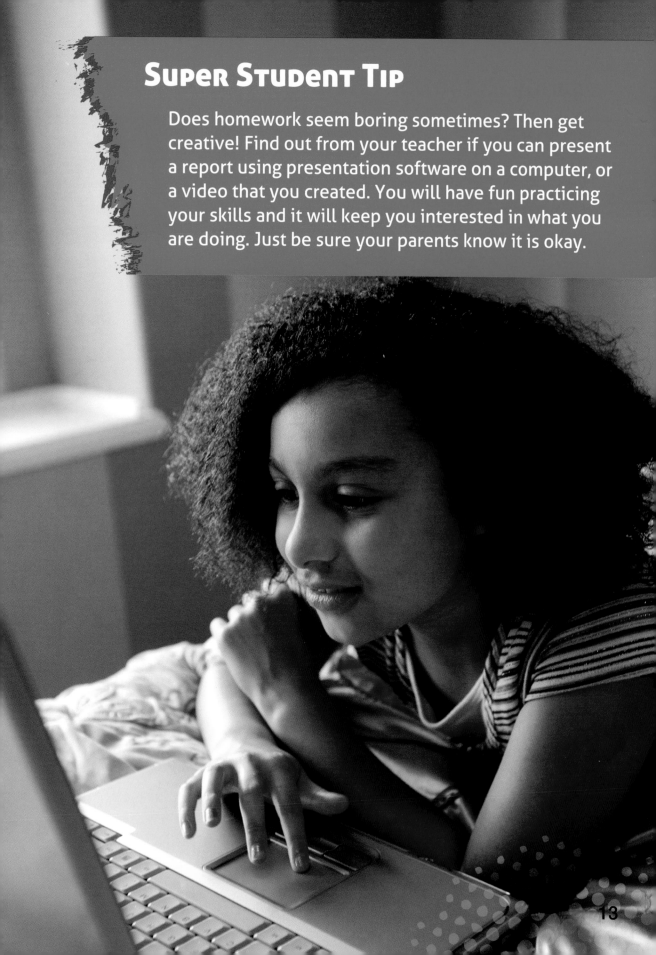

Super Student Tip

Does homework seem boring sometimes? Then get creative! Find out from your teacher if you can present a report using presentation software on a computer, or a video that you created. You will have fun practicing your skills and it will keep you interested in what you are doing. Just be sure your parents know it is okay.

Handy Homework Helpers

Help yourself get your homework done by creating flashcards for basic **memorization**. You can use index cards or cut up paper. Write the problem or word on one side and the answer on the other. Make a STUDY MORE pile, and an I KNOW THIS pile. Keep practicing the study pile until there are no cards left.

Keep flashcards in a special place when you are done with them. You may be able to use them again.

15

One of the best ways to get homework done is by forming or joining a study group. If you have friends in your class who live near you, get together once a week to work on homework or study.

Make a study group more fun with snacks!

Give your friends crunchy, healthy snacks like carrot sticks or pretzels with peanut butter.

OH NO! IT'S TESTING TIME!

Do you have a big test? Relax. Remember, you are not a number or a test score. Don't let one day or one test keep you from reaching your goals.

Make a schedule as far in **advance** of the test as possible. Find out the information that is being tested and how the test will be given. Sometimes, tests are **multiple** choice, short answer, or **essay**.

For a multiple choice test, you can prepare by making flashcards or asking someone to quiz you. When taking a short answer test, be sure to answer using complete sentences that provide as much detail about the question as possible. For an essay test, be sure you can write one or more organized paragraphs. Use your best handwriting.

Use a simple calendar to schedule your plans for studying for a test. If the test is just a simple spelling test, you may not need as many days. If it is at the end of a big unit, you may need to schedule more time.

January Study Schedule

SUN	MON	TUE	WED	THU	FRI	SAT
7	8 Get spelling words and write them three times.	9 Make spelling flashcards.	10 Read Chapter 2 from science book.	11 Have mom help take a practice spelling test.	12 Spelling Test!	13
14	15 Answer questions at the end of the science chapter.	16 Meet with science study group.	17 Review chapter notes for science.	18 Chapter 2 Science Test!	19	20

Standardized Tests

Standardized tests are used in almost every school across the country. They can seem scary, but there are some **strategies** you can use and learn before the test that will help you.

Test-Taking Tips

Before the test:
- Go to bed early the night before.
- Eat breakfast in the morning.
- Plan on being to school early or on time so you can feel organized and not rushed.
- Relax and do not **cram** right before taking a test. What you have learned is stored in your long-term memory.

During the test:
- Be serious and thoughtful.
- For reading tests, try and skim the questions before reading the passage. This will help you recognize information you need while reading.
- Make sure you do not hurry through the test. You may miss a whole question, or make a simple math mistake because of carelessness.
- Make sure not to spend too much time on one question. This could make it hard to finish the test.
- Answer every question no matter what.

After the test:
- Take a deep breath and be glad you did your best. Try not to worry about it anymore.
  Do not go over questions in your mind and wonder about the correct answers.
  Take a break. You deserve it!

Be sure to read for fun and for school every day.
Pay attention in class and ask for help when you need it.

Good study habits, a positive attitude, and the willingness to do your best all the time will pay off later in life. Someday soon, you will be able to have a real job that pays real money and you will be grateful you learned as much as you did in school!

GLOSSARY

advance (ad-VANSS): ahead or before

cram (KRAM): to rush to study before a test

essay (ESS-ay): a longer piece of writing about one topic or theme

goals (GOHLS): plans or events that you work toward to complete

memorization (MEM-ur-uh-zay-shun): the act of learning information so it is not forgotten

multiple (MUHL-tuh-puhl): more than one thing or part

resource (REE-sorss): a useful thing or person to help you

standardized (STAN-durd-ized): made the same for all

strategies (STRAT-uh-jees): smart plans to meet a goal or solve a problem

INDEX

WEBSITES TO VISIT

fit.webmd.com/kids/move/article/good-study-habits

kidshealth.org/kid/feeling/school/homework_help.html

www.scholastic.com/kids/homework/flashcards.htm

ABOUT THE AUTHOR

Meg Greve lives in Chicago with her husband Tom, and her two children, Madison and William. They are always working hard to be a success in school and out of school!

Meet The Author!
www.meetREMauthors.com